Artists in Profile

CONTEMPORARY ARTISTS

Rachel Barnes

www.heinemann.co.uk/library
Visit our website to find out more information about **Heinemann Library** books.

To order:
☎ Phone 44 (0) 1865 888066
▤ Send a fax to 44 (0) 1865 314091
▢ Visit the Heinemann Bookshop at www.heinemann.co.uk/library to browse our catalogue and order online.

First published in Great Britain by Heinemann Library, Halley Court, Jordan Hill, Oxford OX2 8EJ, a division of Reed Educational and Professional Publishing Ltd. Heinemann is a registered trademark of Reed Educational & Professional Publishing Limited.

OXFORD MELBOURNE AUCKLAND JOHANNESBURG BLANTYRE
GABORONE IBADAN PORTSMOUTH NH (USA) CHICAGO

Designed by Tinstar Design (www.tinstar.co.uk)
Originated by Ambassador Litho Ltd
Printed by South China Printing Company, Hong Kong/China

ISBN 0 431 11653 9 (hardback)   ISBN 0 431 11658 X (paperback)
06 05 04 03   07 06 05 04 03
10 9 8 7 6 5 4 3 2   10 9 8 7 6 5 4 3 2 1

British Library Cataloguing in Publication Data
Barnes, Rachel
    Contemporary artists. – (Artists in profile)
    1.Art, Modern – 20th century – Juvenile literature
    I.Title
    709'.04

Acknowledgements
The Publishers would like to thank the following for permission to reproduce photographs:
AKG/ Angelika Platen pp22, 46; AKG/ DACS 2002 pp6, 17; AKG/ Daniel Frasnay p43; AKG/ Niklaus Stauss pp10, 15, 34; AKG/Succession Marcel Duchamp/ADAGP, Paris and DACS, London 2002 p5; Bridgeman/ Private Collection p12; Bridgeman/Leeds Museums And Galleries p25; Camera Press pp37, 38; Camera Press/ Eamonn Mccabe p53; Camera Press/ J.S. Lewinski p31; Camera Press/ James Gray p40; Camera Press/ Janusz Kawa p18; Camera Press/ Richard Stonehouse p28; Corbis/ Christie's Images p44; Corbis/ Julian Calder p27; Corbis/ Michael Nicholson p29; Corbis/ Richard Glover p54; Corbis/ Scott T. Smith p8; Corbis/ Tom Salyer p23; Corbis/Julian Calder p24; National Gallery of Canada, Ottawa p47; Private Collection/ Bridgeman Art Library/ADAGP, Paris and DACS, London 2002 p11; Tate, London 2001 p32; Tate, London 2001/DACS 2002 p35; Tate, London 2002 p50; The Detroit Institute of Arts, USA/Bridgeman Art Library/ Mr & Mrs Walter B. Ford II Fund p41; Ugo Mulas p49; Walker Art Center/Louise Bourgeois/VAGA, New York/DACS, London 2002 p20.

Cover photograph: Andy Goldsworthy

Our thanks to Richard Stemp for his help in the preparation of this book.

Every effort has been made to contact copyright holders of any material reproduced in this book. Any omissions will be rectified in subsequent printings if notice is given to the Publisher.

Contents

Words appearing in the text in bold, **like this**, are explained in the glossary.

What is Contemporary Art?

In more recent years, artists have rebelled against the traditional idea that art is only about painting a picture or making a sculpture to view in a gallery. They say that art can be anything you want it to be and it can be made and displayed anywhere – in a city street, in a field or in a wood, as well as in a studio or a gallery. Contemporary artists make videos, **Installation Art** and **Performance Art** and take photographs.

The desire to open up and challenge the meaning of art, however, is not actually so recent. In 1913, the French artist Marcel Duchamp made a piece of sculpture from a bicycle which the viewer was invited to engage with by turning the wheel around. Duchamp had not actually made it – he had just bought it. He called it a 'ready-made'. In 1918, his ready-made of a urinal was first shown. He put it on display in an exhibition, called it *Fountain* and signed it with the name R. Mutt. Around the same time, he showed a print of Leonardo's famous Mona Lisa with a moustache and a rude slogan drawn on it. Both pieces created a huge scandal which was exactly what Duchamp had wanted. He was deliberately ridiculing people who were too serious, or pretentious, about art. He was also making the point that art is what an artist says it is and something that will make the viewer completely reconsider its meaning.

Dada and Surrealism

At the root of many of the ideas behind contemporary art lies a movement known as **Surrealism** that developed first in literature, and then in art and architecture, during the 1920s and '30s. Surrealism itself arose out of a movement called 'Dada'. This name, meaning 'nonsense', was given to an international group of artists who rebelled against conventional art and the art of the past. Disillusioned by the outcome of World War I with its devastating loss of life and failure to realize their hopes for a better world, artists reacted by rejecting everything that remained of 19th-century academic traditions in art. They delighted in provoking strong feelings with their art.

Surrealism grew out of Dada in Paris in the early 1920s. Artists such as André Masson, Joan Miró and Jean Arp, and later René Magritte and Salvador Dali, explored the workings of the subconscious mind and created absurd, bizarre and dreamlike images in their work.

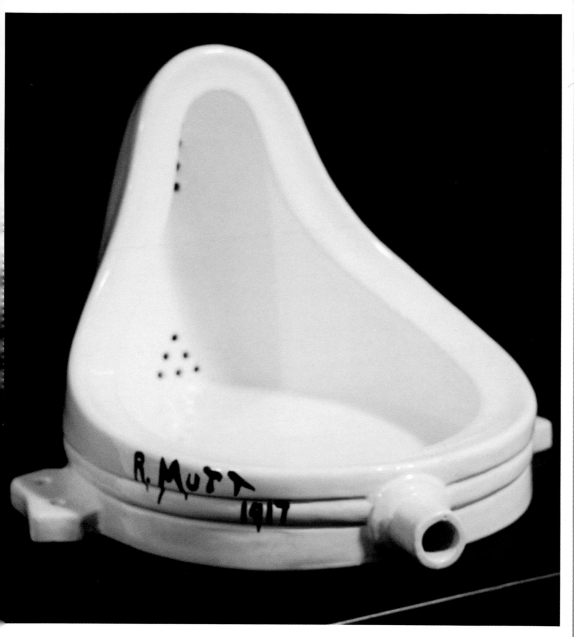

▟ *Fountain*, by Marcel Duchamp (1917)
This 'ready-made', a urinal that Duchamp ordered rather than physically made, caused a huge scandal at the time, as the artist had intended. The use of ready-mades and the debate about the meaning and purpose of art continues a century later.

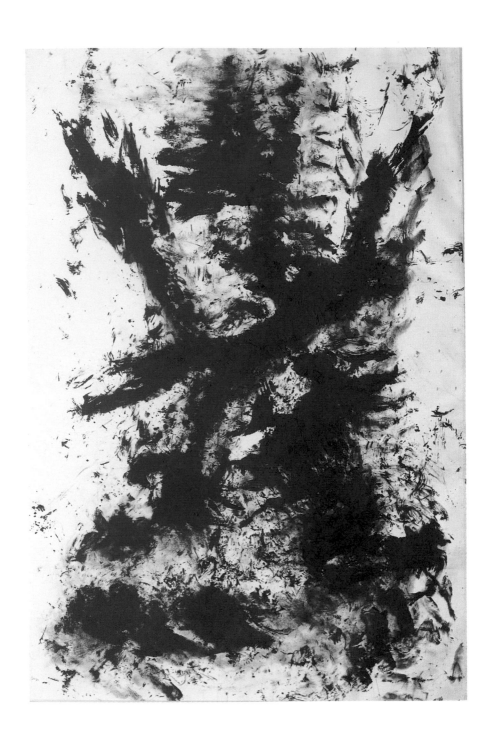

■■ *Anthropometric*, by Yves Klein (1960)
To make this painting, the artist first painted nude models in blue paint, then asked them to lie down and press the paint onto canvas on the floor to create a work where the imprints of the models' bodies made the painting.

Performance Art

One way that contemporary artists have sought to challenge the meaning of art is by Performance Art. Performance Art is an expressive way of freeing artists from the art object itself. The artist, in effect, becomes the object, as he or she performs before an audience who are also encouraged to take part. Dance, music, theatre and mime, as well as fine art, might come into the performance. Performance Art is a continuation of the **'happenings'** of the 1960s.

There was also a huge variety of media, materials and subjects that could be used in Performance Art. One critic described it as 'the most immediate art form ... for it means getting down to the bare bones of aesthetic communication'. One of the very earliest performances was made when the French artist Yves Klein used naked women covered in blue paint as live 'brushes' to paint a picture before an invited audience.

Installation Art

There were some artists of extraordinary gifts and imagination who were genuinely creating a new art form. The poetic genius of the German sculptor and teacher, Joseph Beuys (1921–86), was one of the biggest influences on **Post-modern** art. It was Beuys who was responsible for developing the concept of an installation – that is, an entire room in which the artist places – or installs – whatever they choose to make a display, such as paintings, sculpture, video or photography. It is difficult to find an Installation Artist today who does not feel themselves hugely indebted to Beuys. For example, the German Performance and Installation Artist Rebecca Horn (b. 1945) claims Beuys as her mentor.

From the earliest history of Installation Art, the concept of art as an object to be viewed without calling for any participation from the viewer, as had been the case with traditional art, was questioned and challenged. In Marcel Duchamp's *Bicycle Wheel* (1913) the visitor was asked to spin the wheel around on entering the studio and watch the motion, becoming not merely an observer but a participant. By the late 1960s and the 1970s a number of artists were becoming recognized specifically as Installation Artists.

Outdoor installations

Land Artists, such as Richard Long and Andy Goldsworthy, have rebelled against the idea of making sculptures to be shown in galleries by constructing natural installations in the countryside. They use natural, 'found' materials such as stones and sticks and sometimes whole trees. The resulting structures are sometimes temporary, their existence recorded for posterity by photographs; or sometimes they are permanent, 'growing' into the landscape until they become part of it.

The Bulgarian artist Christo (b. 1935) makes installations in the open air and sometimes on a massive scale, wrapping buildings, surrounding islands with floating plastic skirts and fencing in miles of coastline and inland hills. In the early 1980s, he made one of his masterpieces – *Homage to Claude Monet*, also known as *Surrounded Islands, Biscayne Bay, Florida*. It consisted of

■■■ *Spiral Jetty,* by Robert Smithson (1970)
Smithson not only constructed and photographed this beautiful earthwork, his drawings of the 457 metres long spiral are works of art in their own right.

1.8 million square metres of brilliant pink fabric wrapped around eleven small islands which transformed them into gigantic water-lilies floating on the sea around Florida.

Conceptual Art

In the 1960s artists such as the American Sol LeWitt developed a form of art whereby the idea behind the work was as important, if not more so, than the work itself. In Conceptual Art, the actual physical realization of an idea takes second place to preparatory work relating to the idea that may be carried out, such as sketches, instructions and other texts. Sol LeWitt defined his art form in 1967: 'In Conceptual Art the idea or concept is the most important aspect of the work ... All planning and decisions are made beforehand and the execution is a perfunctory affair. The idea becomes the machine that makes the art.'

Video Art

The first works in the field of **Video Art** were made in response to the increasing popularity of television in the 1960s. In the 1980s the borderline between Video Art and popular commercial video became blurred. In the 1990s, there was a tendency to merge video and computer art. Its combination with sculptural elements has established it as an art form in its own right.

During the 20th century artists have constantly evolved and reinvented themselves in a huge variety of ways. This book will look at those contemporary artists who have taken their work out of the gallery and into the surrounding city streets, parks and countryside so that it can be seen by as many people as possible.

Institute of Contemporary Arts (ICA)

An organization that has done much to promote contemporary art is the Institute of Contemporary Arts in London. The ICA was established in 1947 by Roland Penrose and Herbert Read. It describes itself as 'a public playground for developing and presenting new and challenging work across the arts; for forging innovative ways of thinking about the wider culture; and for experimenting with the presentation of the arts'. It is a non-profit-making institution and an educational charity, financially assisted by the Arts Council of England, Westminster City Council and the British Film Institute. The ICA puts on exhibitions by new artists from all over the world, films, live events, debates and club nights.

Jean-Michel Basquiat 1960–88

- Born in Brooklyn, New York, on 22 December 1960.
- Died in New York City on 12 August 1988.

Key works

K, 1982
Napoleonic Stereotype, 1983
Zydeco, 1984

The talented and wayward Jean-Michel Basquiat is a famous example of the gifted, self-destructive artist who burned himself out young. He was born on 22 December 1960 in Brooklyn, New York. His father Gerard was a middle-class accountant from Haiti and his mother Matilde was of Puerto Rican descent. Basquiat was bilingual in Spanish and English and, as a child, loved to read. He also showed an early interest in drawing, which his mother encouraged, often taking him on trips to the Metropolitan Museum of Art and the Museum of Modern Art in New York.

■■ *Handsome, flamboyant and extrovert, Basquiat was a familiar figure in the New York art scene during his tragically brief life.*

However, two traumas in early childhood marked Basquiat deeply. The first was in May 1968 when he was knocked over by a car while playing in the street. It was a serious accident – his arm was broken and he had to have his spleen removed. He was in hospital for a month. His mother brought him a copy of the medical encyclopedia, *Gray's Anatomy*, which has detailed anatomical drawings. This book had a lasting impact on his work. In the same year he experienced his second trauma. His parents split up and his father retained custody of Basquiat and his two sisters. Basquiat was always much closer to his mother than to his father, so it was especially painful for him not to live with her.

When Basquiat was fourteen and already becoming a rebellious teenager, Gerard Basquiat took him and his two sisters to Puerto Rico, where they stayed for two years. It was from this time onwards that Basquiat's pattern of rebelling and running away began. When he was sixteen, the family went back to New York. Here, his father put him in City-as-School, a special school for gifted children with learning difficulties that was designed to use the city's museums as the basis for teaching. Although the school was liberal, Basquiat still felt the need to run away from home. On one occasion, after he had been missing for two weeks, his father discovered him in Washington Square Park in Greenwich Village, where he had spent much of his time taking the drug LSD.

Basquiat did make an important friendship at City-as-School. Al Diaz was a member of an informal teenage group of **graffiti** artists in New York, and introduced Basquiat to the movement. Basquiat and Diaz invented a fictional character SAMO (Same Old Shit) with whose name they signed their huge (illicit) works of graffiti on New York subways and streets. Already, while still at school, Diaz and Basquiat were attracting attention from the press.

Basquiat's school days came to an end in June 1977. He disrupted the graduation ceremonies at his school by throwing shaving cream all over the principal's head. A year later he left home for good, with his father's reluctant agreement. He had nowhere to live and either slept on the floor of friends' flats or rough on the streets. He was already starting to use Class A drugs, such as heroin and cocaine.

Success, by Jean-Michel Basquiat (1980)
Basquiat's Success uses the colours and stylization of street graffiti in a mix of personal icons.

Basquiat had taken to dressing in exotic and outlandish clothes and soon became a familiar figure on the down-town club scene at the East Village Mudd Club. He loved partying and wild dancing and for a while fell out with his friend Diaz, who was suspicious that Basquiat's attention-seeking behaviour was blatant self-advertising. Basquiat had taken over the use of the SAMO tag. In 1979, now aged nineteen, he formed his own band, which went under many different names including 'Noise Band'. He also produced T-shirts, drawings and **collages**, which he sold in Washington Square Park and also in front of the Museum of Modern Art.

Untitled, by Jean-Michel Basquiat (1984)
Basquiat's graffiti art, initially painted on the walls of the New York subway, derived from a number of sources, but was essentially figurative.

Basquiat's breakthrough came in 1980 when he exhibited his artwork for the first time in the 'Times Square Show'. This was a group exhibition held in a vacant building in New York. It was a big success. Basquiat, who at this crucial point was introduced to the famous **Pop Artist** Andy Warhol, decided to leave his band and become a full-time artist. Warhol, who was initially wary of Basquiat, was to become an important influence for him.

From this time Basquiat showed his work frequently, attracting attention not just locally in New York but further afield in Europe, where his status rose as an exciting representative of mixed-race urban culture. In May 1981, he had his first solo show at the Galleria d'Arte Emilio Mazzola in Modena, Italy, and in September 1981 an Italian art dealer with a gallery in New York, Annina Nosei, became his first art dealer. An enthusiastic article in *Artforum*, a leading art magazine, helped to consolidate his growing fame.

Basquiat had achieved all he had dreamed of. He was famous on his own terms for his own highly original art. In 1983, when he was only 23 years old, he was included in the **Whitney Biennial Exhibition** in New York, a huge mark of recognition. Basquiat's use of both heroin and cocaine was now excessive and his behaviour as a result was becoming disturbingly wild and unpredictable. He fell out with friends and art dealers, never keeping one for long. It was said by many of his friends that his relationship with Warhol was one of the few stabilizing influences in his chaotic life, even though this too was problematic. Basquiat was devastated when Warhol died quite suddenly in 1987. He quickly slipped into an increasingly self-destructive spiral. He died at the age of 27 on 12 August 1988 from a massive drugs overdose, in his studio in Great Jones Street Loft, New York.

Keith Haring

Keith Haring was born on 4 May 1958 in Reading, Pennsylvania. Like Basquiat he became renowned for his work as a graffiti artist. Haring, however, had studied the visual arts and been taught drawing, painting, sculpture and art history at the School of Visual Arts in New York. It was while he was in New York that he became friends with Basquiat. Together they enjoyed the 'scene', especially the graffiti scene, in East Village. Haring said, 'Graffiti were the most beautiful things I ever saw.'

Haring had his first show in October 1982 at the Tony Shafrazi Gallery in New York. The show was very successful and made Haring's name on New York's art scene. His success continued until his name was known globally. Sadly, Keith Haring died of AIDS on 16 February 1990. He was only 31 years old.

Joseph Beuys 1921–86

- Born in Krefeld, Germany, on 12 May 1921.
- Died in Dusseldorf, Germany, on 23 January 1986.

Key works
Bed, 1950
Felt Suit, 1970
The Revolution is Us, 1972

Joseph Beuys, **Performance Artist**, sculptor, **Installation Artist** and teacher, was arguably one of the greatest influences on **Post-modern** European art. He was born in Krefeld in Germany on 12 May 1921. He spent his childhood and adolescence at Rindern, near Cleves, in Germany. This was where his father, from whom he was always very distant, had a flour and fodder business. Joseph's family were Roman Catholic. He was an only child and exceptionally inquisitive. He was passionately interested in science and the natural world (he built a laboratory in his parents' house), local history, folk tales and mythology. He was a very musical child – he played the piano and the cello. He was also beginning to nurture a passionate interest in anything to do with art and regularly visited the studio of a local sculptor called Achilles Moortgat. His later work reflected these early interests: virtually everything he did told a part of his life story.

He wanted to become a paediatrician (children's doctor) after leaving school, but World War II prevented him from doing this. In 1940, aged nineteen, he joined Hitler's *Luftwaffe*, the German airforce, as a dive bomber pilot, stationed in Southern Russia, the Ukraine and the Crimea. The most lasting influence on his entire artistic career was a traumatic event he suffered during this time. According to his own account (and this has been questioned), while serving as a *Luftwaffe* fighter pilot in 1943, he was shot down and given up for dead in the blizzard-swept Crimea. His life was saved by local Tartar tribesmen who throughout the war went on with their lives, disdainful of Soviet and German armies alike. They found Beuys's frozen and shattered body and proceeded to smother him in fat and wrap him in felt to keep him insulated and warm.

Although he was unconscious for much of this traumatic experience, it left an indelible mark on him. For the rest of his life Beuys used these precious materials, fat and felt, in his work. For him they were symbols of energy and warmth and represented the means of his survival. In a performance piece in 1965, he piled asymmetrical clumps of animal grease in empty rooms and then wrapped himself in fat and grease, an act that ritualized the materials and techniques employed by his rescuers in the Crimea.

After the war, in 1946, Beuys returned to Cleves and decided to become a sculptor. He studied privately with Walter Brux, a local Cleves artist, and then in 1947 at the Düsseldorf Academy, although he continued to suffer from the aftermath of his wartime experiences. He graduated from the academy in 1952 and spent much of the 1950s focusing on drawing rather than sculpture.

In 1961 he joined the sculpture faculty at the Kunstakademie in Düsseldorf as Professor of Monumental Sculpture. Determined to restore a human element to both art and politics, Beuys later said that he began at this time to view his works 'as stimulants for the transformation of the idea of sculpture or of art in general'. In particular he wanted to provoke discussion and stimulate ideas about what art can be and how the concept of art-making may be 'extended to the visible materials used by everyone'.

Briefly, between 1962 and 1965, Beuys joined **Fluxus**, a loosely knit, non-comformist group largely inspired by artist Marcel Duchamp and musician John Cage, noted for their **happenings**, mixed media events, publications and concerts. But by the end of 1965, Beuys decided to leave, saying that 'they held a mirror up to people without indicating how to change anything', that is, they showed society its faults but did not offer any ways of improvement. In a defiant act of rebellion before he left, Beuys scribbled the words 'The silence of Marcel Duchamp is overrated' on the blackboard.

■ ■ ■ The German born Beuys was a charismatic and mysterious character who had a huge influence on experimental art.

One of Beuys's most extraordinarily poetic and mysterious works was a performance piece, originally enacted at Düsseldorf's Schelma Gallery in 1965, entitled *How to Explain Pictures to a Dead Hare*. For this piece, Beuys sat or strode about in an empty room surrounded by his familiar media of felt, fat, wire and wool. With his head covered in honey, laced with gold leaf, he cradled a dead hare in his arms, which he murmured to in a barely audible whisper. The artist also had a magnetized iron plate tied to his right foot so that he noisily clanked around the room as he whispered to the dead hare. Later he said that he was stressing, 'the problem of explaining things, particularly where art and creative work are concerned. Even a dead animal preserves more power of intuition than some human beings with their stubborn rationality.'

Beuys was interested in an astonishingly wide range of ideas and subjects. He created a very varied body of work in different media and to different scales, including drawings, prints, sculptures, performances and installations. His drawings were always very important to him. They often acted as points of departure for later work, frequently containing the seeds of ideas that would evolve into sculptures, lectures or performances. At the same time, drawing was vital to him as a fundamental, expressive and cathartic (cleansing) process in itself. Beuys was first and foremost a communicator, in his own highly individual and mystical way. Through his works, he wanted to spread his ideas about art being an essential part of everyday life. He wanted also to express his emotions – anxiety, joy, love, anger and fear.

Although a radical artist in his early life, later on Beuys became a central figure in the art world. In the 1960s he participated in marches and protests. His belief that every human being should be considered a student and allowed to attend classes, led to him being dismissed from his teaching position at the Düsseldorf Academy in 1972. He was always absorbed in political issues for society, which led to his co-founding of the Green Party in Germany in 1979.

When Beuys died of heart failure in Düsseldorf on 23 January 1986, many were surprised to learn that he was survived by a wife, Eva (whom he had married in 1959), and two children. He had lived such a strange and extraordinarily independent life, and had also always been so secretive about his private life, that these signs of a more normal, conventional existence seemed out of character.

■■ *Felt Suit*, by Joseph Beuys (1970)
After the traumatic experience of being shot down and given up for
dead whilst serving as a fighter pilot in 1943, much of Beuys' art,
such as this felt suit, relates to the time his life was subsequently saved
by local Tartar tribesmen. The suit represents comfort, warmth and
preservation rather than being an object of beauty.

Louise Bourgeois b. 1911

- Born in Paris on 24 December 1911.
- Has lived in New York, USA, since 1938.

Key works
The Destruction of the Father, 1973
Cell (Eyes and Mirrors), 1989
Woman and Suitcase, 1994

Louise Bourgeois is motivated by an intensely personal, autobiographical approach to her work, strongly influenced by her traumatic childhood. She has worked in a wide range of media, from wood and stone to latex and rubber. Bourgeois was born in Paris on 24 December 1911. Her parents' occupation was restoring tapestries, which is how as a young girl Bourgeois's interest in making art was awakened and stimulated. 'It taught me that art was interesting and it can be useful,' she later said of this formative time. Her first artistic assignment was to redraw a foot, contained in the lower border of a tapestry which was the part that often rotted away. Bourgeois had an older sister and a younger brother. She said later that she was her father's favourite because she looked like him. It was a complex relationship, however: 'My father would often make me feel small,' she said. 'Teasing, you see, is a permissive form of cruelty.'

But more negative forces were also at work. Her father began an affair with the children's English governess, Sadie, who was only a few years older than they were. All three children became implicated in preserving the delicate balance of relations between father, mother and mistress as the affair was conducted within the family home. Bourgeois's mother became ill with the lung disease emphysema and, from 1922 to 1932, the family spent the winters in the South of France for the sake of her health. Sadie, the governess, always accompanied them. 'My mind as an artist was conditioned by that affair, by my jealousy of that dreadful intruder. I learned that the way to survive is to make yourself indispensable to someone else. My father needed me. I pleased him. I was never rejected. But it made me feel sad.'

Bourgeois's mother died in 1932 and she mourned her deeply. Her father teased her about her grief to the extent that she tried to drown herself – he had to leap into the river and rescue her. Her mother's death was a major turning point in her life: 'When she died ... this rage to understand took me over. If you fear abandonment, it keeps you in a fear of dependency, which makes you feel unable to cope.'

An extraordinary woman still making exciting art in her nineties, Bourgeois had to wait a very long time before receiving international recognition for her art.

Bourgeois decided to study mathematics at the Sorbonne University in Paris as she thought it was a safe, reliable subject, but she quickly became disillusioned. She enrolled as an art student at the **École des Beaux-Arts**, and trained under the French **Cubist** painter Fernand Léger. **Surrealism** was becoming popular at this time and the young student met many Surrealist artists, who were to have a major influence on her work. But Bourgeois has always seen her art as fundamentally different: 'I do not regard myself as a Surrealist because I have never mentioned the word dream in discussing my art, while they talked about the dream all the time. I don't dream. You might say I work under a spell and I truly value the spell.'

In 1938, Bourgeois married the American art historian Robert Goldwater, who she would later claim held an immediate attraction for her as he could stand up to her father. 'I married first of all an intellectual. He was interested in nothing but ideas. That means he was interested in what is true and what is not true,' she says of him. They adopted a son, Michel, and moved to New York, where she has remained ever since, becoming an American citizen in 1951. She studied art in New York and became friends with artists such as Marcel Duchamp, Le Corbusier, Joan Miró and Andy Warhol.

▓▓ *The Blind Leading the Blind*, by Louise Bourgeois (1989)
Bourgeois has worked in a wide variety of materials and disciplines.
This wooden sculpture refers, like much of her work, to her traumatic
childhood and her love–hate relationship with her father.

Bourgeois and her husband had two sons in America, but she was also starting to build herself a career as an artist. During the years of World War II, she worked at the **Art Students' League** in New York. Her first solo show as a painter took place in 1945 and in 1949 she had her first exhibition of sculpture at the Peridot Gallery in New York. Although she was beginning to receive some recognition, it was still necessary for her to teach to supplement her income.

It was not until the 1970s, however, that the artistic climate changed sufficiently to accept Bourgeois's work. The **feminist movement**, which she herself supported, was also gathering power at this time and was crucial in recognizing Bourgeois's unique contribution as painter, printmaker, sculptor, **installation** and **performance** artist. In 1973 her husband Robert Goldwater died, which meant that Bourgeois had to change the focus of her life. She joined the feminist movement and took part in art-political demonstrations. Although Bourgeois had shown her work in a number of exhibitions since the 1940s, it was her first solo **retrospective** exhibition at the Museum of Modern Art in New York in 1982 that finally launched her extraordinary late career.

Now in her 90s, Bourgeois is philosophical both about her early years with no recognition and her more recent meteoric rise to fame. 'I have ridden out my success because it was not really the purpose of my work to be successful,' she says. 'My work will outlive its success, be more enduring and stronger than success. I was never disappointed when I never had success which is why I never destroyed any of my work.'

Cindy Sherman

Sherman was born on 19 January 1954 in Glen Ridge, New Jersey, USA. She studied painting and photography at the State University College, Buffalo, where she obtained her BA degree in 1976. She started to develop her highly original way of expressing herself in her early college days.

For her art, Sherman dresses up as different female characters, often **stereotypes** of how women are portrayed in the media, in films or on television, and then takes photographs of herself as these characters. The photographs are not typical self-portraits because Sherman is not playing herself. Like that of Bourgeois, Sherman's work is often termed as 'feminist' because of the way her photographs seem to challenge the traditional male view of women. She continues to live and work in New York.

Christo b. 1935

- Born in Gabrovno, Bulgaria on 13 June 1935.
- Lived in Paris from 1958 to 1964, when he emigrated to the USA.

Key works

Wrapped Coast – One Million Square Feet (Little Bay, Australia), 1969
Valley Curtain (Rifle, Colorado), 1972
Running Fence, 1976

Although he was initially a painter, Christo became world famous in the 1960s when he invented '**empaquetage**' – surrounding objects in materials such as canvas or semi-transparent plastic.

Christo Javacheff was born in Gabrovno in Bulgaria on 13 June 1935. His father was an engineer chemist who ran a textile factory. Christo studied at the Academy in Sofia, Bulgaria, from 1952 to 1956. After brief periods in Prague, Vienna (where he studied sculpture), and Geneva, he moved to Paris in 1958. Here he earned his living as a portrait painter before he had the idea of empaquetage. He began with small objects such as paint tins from his studio, but the objects became more and more ambitious and ranged from trees and motor cars to buildings and sections of landscape.

An eccentric, yet very committed artist, Christo has enjoyed international fame with his 'empaquetage' – his wrapping of objects, buildings, and landscapes.

In Paris, Christo married Jeanne-Claude Guillebon, who would collaborate with him on all his projects. They had a son, Cyril, in 1960. In 1961 Christo had his first one-man show at the Hero Lauhus Gallery, Cologne. The family emigrated to the United States in 1964.

Christo and Jeanne-Claude's ventures of wrapping landscape include *Running Fence*, a fence that meanders through California for a distance of 39 kilometres (1976). The couple spend huge amounts of time negotiating permission for their projects, financing them with the sale of smaller works of art. Christo and Jeanne-Claude do not accept grants or sponsorships for their work and because their artworks are in public spaces they do not receive payment from those who come to see them. Their projects can be expensive. Sometimes Christo needs to hire large teams of specialists, such as professional rock climbers and engineers. The total cost of making *Running Fence* was $3.2 million.

In Christo's work the preparation, such as studies of the site and preliminary drawings, is an inherent part of the work. Often included is a study of the impact on the environment that the project will have. The whole process can be extremely lengthy; the wrapping of the Reichstag in Berlin, for example, took 26 years from start to finish (1971–95). A photographic record of the key stages was made by Wolfgang Volz. Christo and Jeanne-Claude always remove all traces of their art from the site so all that is left are the photographs.

Christo and Jeanne-Claude still live in the same house they moved into when they emigrated to the USA in 1964.

▌▌ *Surrounded Islands Project*, by Christo (1983)
In one of his most ambitious projects of the 1980s, Christo wrapped miles of coastline around these islands.

Andy Goldsworthy b. 1956

- Born in Cheshire, England, in 1956.
- Now lives in Dumfriesshire, Scotland.

Key works
Balanced Rocks, 1978
Maple Leaf Lines, 1987
Leadgate Maze, 1989

Andy Goldsworthy is a 'land' or 'earth' artist, someone who works within nature. He uses natural materials in natural shapes and forms set in natural contexts. Much of his work is not made to endure, so that taking photographs of his land installations is the only way of keeping a record.

An artist with great charm and originality, Goldsworthy's art has always been directly inspired by nature and natural objects.

Goldsworthy was born in 1956 in Cheshire but brought up in Yorkshire. He studied at Harrogate High School, Bradford College of Art and Preston Polytechnic, where he graduated in 1978 with a BA in Fine Art. Goldsworthy has lived mainly in Britain, in Bentham and Ilkley in Yorkshire, Brough in Cumbria, and Penpont in Dumfriesshire, Scotland, where he lives now.

Conical Leafwork, by Andy Goldsworthy (1988)
Fragile and delicate, these beautiful shapes are highly textural, evoking images of trees and forests.

As a young student Goldsworthy spent much of his time outside college, working on the beaches at Morecambe and Heysham. He was frequently in trouble at College for not attending all the classes, but in actual fact he was already developing important ideas for his **Land Art**.

Many of his works have been sited in the North of England. The giant maze and Lambton Earthwork in County Durham was made in 1988, the Griezedale Forest site works in 1984, the Lake District National Park in 1988. Goldsworthy has worked in many parts of the world, such as Italy (at the **Venice Biennale**), Grise Fiord in the Northern Territories of Canada, the North Pole, Japan, Castres in France, the Australian Outback and Haarlem in Holland. He has had one-man shows in France, Japan, Holland and the UK and participated in group shows in Italy, Germany and the USA. A major **retrospective**, 'Hand to Earth Andy Goldsworthy; Sculpture 1976–1990', was held at the Henry Moore Centre for the Study of Sculpture, Leeds.

David Nash

David Nash, along with Andy Goldsworthy and Richard Long, has been a key figure in British Land Art. Nash was born in Esher, Surrey, in 1945. During the years 1963 to 1967 he studied at Kingston School of Art, before he moved to Blaenau Ffestiniog, in North Wales to get away from the 'unnecessarily competitive' life of the city. From his studio in a former chapel he was able to explore the forms of nature and incorporate them into his work. Nash is fascinated by wood and his works are predominantly made of this material. He makes sculptures out of whole limbs and trunks of trees that have fallen or been uprooted. These are often set in the rugged Welsh countryside that surrounds Nash's studio.

His latest works involve growing and living sculptures in which he coaxes trees or groups of trees to take particular shapes. His famous *Ash Dome* project consists of a 9-metre circle of 22 ash trees that form a domed space more than 5 metres high. Planted in 1977 during a gloomy economic and political period, Nash's intention was to show faith in the future – that by the 21st century when the trees had grown, the world would be a better place. Nash has also recently used fire to transform wood into carbon and air, to create warped shapes in deep cuts in wood. In 1999, Nash was elected to the Royal Academy. He has had more than 80 solo exhibitions all over the world in his 30-year career.

In a recent interview Goldsworthy described his feelings about what he was trying to do in his art. 'The term "landscape" is like "portrait"; it is an expression of distancing; here I am and there it is. But what has been happening in the last twenty years or so is that artists have been getting right in there. Saying no, it is not out there. It is here. We want to make our images with what is here. That is why it is called land art rather than landscape art, "scape" denoting distancing.'

In 1989, Goldsworthy travelled to the North Pole where he made walls of ice, a project which like all Goldsworthy's work was an attempt to achieve an understanding of nature as a process. With the exception of his large projects in open country, such as Leadgate Maze in 1989, his works are temporary and are only preserved by photographs and preparatory sketches. The materials he uses – twigs, leaves, snow, ice, reeds and thorns – are those that he finds in the environment and they often add to the ephemeral (temporary) quality of his work. Some of the material Goldsworthy uses in his work, such as the chalk for the series of arches he made in Goodwood in 1995, are semi-permanent. These arches are now kept indoors to help extend their life, in Goldsworthy's studio in Dumfriesshire where he lives and works.

▮▮▮ *Snow Sculptures*, by Andy Goldsworthy (c. 1980s–2000)
Not all Goldsworthy's work is destined to last! This photograph records his land art in the North Pole where he made walls of ice.

Anthony Gormley b. 1950

- Born in London in 1950.
- Has always lived in London.

Key works
Untitled (For Francis), 1986
Angel of the North, 1998
Quantum Cloud, 2000

Anthony Gormley is a sculptor who creates his work by encasing his body in plaster to make a mould and then casting the mould in lead. This is a difficult and dangerous process, but by doing it he attempts to understand better his relationship with his own body.

▐▐ *After winning the Turner Prize in 1994, Gormley has received international acclaim for his sculptures of the human form.*

He was born in London in 1950. Although he was always very interested in art, as a child he was also very able academically. From 1968 to 1971 he studied anthropology and archaeology and then art history at Trinity College Cambridge. By the time he left, he had decided he did not want merely to study art, but he wanted to become an artist himself. Before he began more studies he travelled to many countries, including Turkey, Syria, Afghanistan, Pakistan and India. On his return in 1974, he went to London and studied at the Central School of Art and Design, Goldsmiths College and finally, from 1977 to 1979, Slade School of Art.

In 1981, Gormley had his first one-man show at the Whitechapel Art Gallery in London. For this show he made his work *Bed*, a 'mattress' of sliced white bread eaten-out into the shape of the body. The same year, assisted by his wife, the painter Vicken Parsons, Gormley began to make moulds from his body which he used as the basis for lead body cases. Gormley wraps himself in a 'prison' of cling film, **scrim** and plaster, from which a fibreglass mould is made; this is then cast in lead or iron and put in place. An example of this technique can be seen in his work *Total Strangers*, made for the town of Cologne, Germany in 1997.

Gormley's work attracted international recognition and he was chosen to represent his country at the **Venice Biennale** in 1984. In 1989, he received widespread recognition for *Field*. This piece is a great expanse of 35,000 miniature terracotta figures made by a family of professional brickmakers in Mexico. It represents a move away from his previous technique of using his own body to make the mould for his sculpture.

Gormley's work is seen to deal with the universal themes of culture and nature, and life and death. In the 1990s his work received an increasing amount of attention, particularly after 1994, when he won the **Turner Prize** with *The Essential Gesture*. In 1998 he made his hugely ambitious sculpture *Angel of the North*. At the time this was the tallest sculpture in Britain. *Angel of the North* is 19.8 metres high, has a wing span of 51.5 metres and weighs approximately 100 tonnes. It was made in three separate parts from weathered steel and stands at the head of the Team Valley, near Gateshead. Gormley still lives and works in London.

▮▮ *The Angel of the North*, by Anthony Gormley (1998)
The tallest sculpture in Britain, Gormley's Angel at the head of the Team Valley, near Gateshead has a wing span of 51.5 metres. Like much of Gormley's work it is a dramatic piece which was made for a particular site.

Barbara Hepworth 1903–75

- Born in Wakefield, Yorkshire, on 10 January 1903.
- Died in a fire in her studio in St Ives, Cornwall, on 20 May 1975.

Key works
Three Forms, 1934
Curved Form, 1956
Hollow Form with Inner Form, 1968

Barbara Hepworth is one of the greatest modern artists to come from the UK. She made **abstract** sculptures inspired by nature from wood, stone and later bronze. She was born in Wakefield, Yorkshire, on 10 January 1903. She was the eldest of four daughters. Her father was a civil engineer who worked in the West Riding of Yorkshire. Hepworth was close to her father and through him became familiar with technical drawing. Her understanding of her father's work was aided by her talent for mathematics. At the age of seven, during a slide lecture on Egypt given by the headmistress in her school in Wakefield, Barbara was already thinking of becoming a sculptor.

Hepworth experimented in the darkness of her parents' cellar: clay was not allowed upstairs. Sometimes her father would take her on long, silent car rides through the Pennines. She loved the loneliness and melancholy of the landscape. Even then she was making a connection between sculpture and the land. 'I cannot write anything about landscape without writing about the human figure and human spirit inhabiting the landscape,' she wrote.

Hepworth went to Leeds School of Art in 1920 to study sculpture. She finished the course in one year instead of the usual two. It was there she met Henry Moore, who later said that they had 'a bit of an affair'. The mutually beneficial artistic relationship they developed at this time was of vital importance to the future development of both sculptors. It is difficult now to assess who had which idea first at this crucial period of experimentation.

In 1921, Hepworth went to the Royal College of Art on a three-year senior **scholarship**. In 1924 she was a finalist for the Prix de Rome (a competition to choose art students to attend the Académie de France in Rome, Italy). The winner of this prize was John Skeaping, who was to become her husband. Hepworth received a grant from the West Riding to live and travel in Italy for a year. She and Skeaping married in the Palazzo Vecchio, Florence, before going on to Siena and then to Rome, where she trained as a carver.

■■ *Photographed towards the end of her life, in her studio in St Ives, where she later died in a fire, Hepworth touches one of her carved sculptures inspired by the Cornish landscape.*

Hepworth and Skeaping returned to London in November 1926. The following year they held a joint exhibition in their studio in St John's Wood. In 1929 their son Paul was born. They divorced in 1931, and in the same year while on a group holiday, Hepworth met the artist Ben Nicholson, destined to be her next husband.

In 1931, Hepworth went to live with Nicholson in Hampstead, London. She gave birth to triplets (Simon, Rachel and Sarah) in November 1934. Hepworth and Nicholson were married on 17 November 1936. Nicholson introduced her to Pablo Picasso and Jean Arp and there was a constant exchange of ideas. In pre-war London, the couple shared their home with other artists including Paul Nash, Piet Mondrian, Naum Gabo and Walter Gropius. The Russian sculptor Gabo was also crucial to Hepworth's development. He introduced her to the use of strings in sculpture, which she employed to brilliant effect to capture movement in her sculpture *Stringed Figure-Curlew*.

Pelagos, by Barbara Hepworth (1946)
The curving, undulating form, with its light blue inside appears directly inspired by the huge crashing breakers on the Altantic coast in Cornwall, where the artist made this sculpture.

Although not always an instigator of ideas, Hepworth was adept at incorporating a new idea from someone else, making it a part of her own style. However, she was conceivably the first to use a hole in her *Pierced Form* (1931). It was a tremendous breakthrough – quite literally! 'I felt the most intense pleasure in piercing the stone to make an **abstract** form and space,' she later recalled. Her final effortless transition from **figurative** to abstract form did not happen until 1934. The simple purity and ceaseless flow of line in *Three Forms* (1935) shows how quickly she adapted to non-figurative form, finding it her most natural means of expression.

Hepworth and Nicholson shared difficult, impoverished years during World War II in St Ives, Cornwall, with their triplets in a tiny cottage. They struggled to find space to work. Yet both blossomed artistically in this period. Hepworth missed Nicholson when he left in 1949 to live with another woman, and was seemingly in love with him until the last. They divorced in 1951.

Hepworth lived the rest of her life in Cornwall, where she did her best work, inspired by the landscape and seascape of St Ives and the Penwith peninsula. Prophetically in 1933, before she had ever set foot in Cornwall, the critic J.D. Bernal had compared her work to the neolithic **menhirs** there. Her inspirational pieces of the 1940s and 50s in St Ives, such as the lyrical *Pelagos* and *Wave*, convey her obsession with the ebb and flow of the Atlantic. The sea was always a major inspiration in her work.

Despite major exhibitions at home and abroad, public commissions and academic honours, Hepworth felt bitter on occasions about the way in which her past lover, friend and fellow student Moore was praised to her detriment. At the 1950 **Venice Biennale**, Moore was cited as the master, Hepworth merely the pupil. In more recent years this perception has radically changed, her work, of course being the most important evidence that Hepworth was always a gifted and original artist in her own right.

In 1964, Hepworth was diagnosed with cancer. Her importance in the artistic community was recognized in 1965 when she was made Dame Barbara Hepworth by the Queen. In her last years, with her health failing, she had to take to a wheelchair. Despite this, she went on working whenever she was able. She died in a fire in her studio in St Ives on 20 May 1975. She was 72 years old.

Rebecca Horn b. 1944

- Born in Michelstadt, Germany, on 24 March 1944.
- Has lived mainly in Hamburg and Berlin, Germany.

Key works
Ballet of the Woodpeckers, 1986
Orlando, 1988
Concert for Anarchy, 1990

Rebecca Horn uses a variety of media, including sculpture, **kinetic** installations, **Performance Art** and more recently feature films. From her earliest beginnings as an artist, she has enjoyed the freedom of moving effortlessly between the disciplines.

Horn was born on 24 March 1944 in Germany, just before the end of World War II. She now vividly remembers how history lessons were taught with a strong emphasis on German achievement in those post-war years: 'One of the most extraordinary things immediately after the war was having a German history lesson in school. After 1932, nothing was mentioned; it was as if the time didn't exist.'

▇▇▇ *Horn's dramatic beauty became known through her performance pieces in the 1970s and then later in her art films in the 1990s.*

From 1964 to 1970, she attended the Higher Institute for Fine Art in Hamburg. As a young student in the late 1960s, she became seriously ill after inhaling toxic fumes from the polyester and fibreglass she was using to make her sculptures. 'Nobody told us that it was poisonous,' she says. 'I was in the sanatorium for almost a year, and ill for a long time afterwards. It was a nightmare and I often felt like jumping out of the window. Both my parents died at this time and I felt completely isolated and unconnected with everything. Perhaps I had to make something positive out of the suffering to survive.'

Although reluctant to speak of this painful time, she now realizes that it was a turning point. 'I started to make an inner fantasy world; to escape from the outside world which I could not bear ... Often I would get this burning feeling inside and my imagination ran riot with absurd, wonderful thoughts and ideas.'

At this time she began making body extensions out of soft materials, such as cloth, hair and later feathers, which were reminiscent of bandages and prostheses (artifical body parts). She described these body extensions as 'a kind of cocoon to protect myself'. Although her imaginary world developed during her illness, she recognizes that it began in her childhood: 'As a little girl my parents were always worried about what I would come up with next,' she says.

Horn lived in Hamburg until 1971. She continued making her body extensions but began to incorporate them into performances. Her first large-scale public performance was in 1971 when, during a stay in London, she was invited to take part in the 'Documenta' exhibition in Kassel. But it was not until 1973, when living in West Berlin, that she had her first solo exhibition at the Galerie René Block. Horn also made her first film, *Berlin Exercises: Dreaming Under Water*, which won a prize in 1975.

Today, Rebecca Horn is an internationally famous artist, staging her exhibitions all over Europe. She still lives in Germany where she also teaches at the Akademie der Kunst in Berlin.

Ballet of the Woodpeckers, by Rebecca Horn (1986)
This eerie installation makes use of mirrors and the sound of repeated tapping against them to conjure up the sound of the woodpeckers. It has a quite sinister empty feeling which relates to her long stay in a sanitorium as a young woman.

Yves Klein 1928–62

- Born in Nice, France on 28 April 1928.
- Died in Paris on 6 June 1962 of a heart attack.

Key works
Do-Do-Do Blue, 1960
Leap into the Void, 1960
FC -11 Anthropometry-Fire, 1961

Yves Klein helped to change the course of the art world by stressing the importance not of a piece of art but of the artist as a personality. He was born in Nice, France, on 28 April 1928. His parents – both artists – were **bohemians** and totally wrapped up in their own lives. They completely failed to provide a secure home life for their son. This was left up to a childless aunt who was more stable and respectable, but also possessive and smothering. The careless parents and demanding aunt between them sent very mixed and confusing messages to the young, sensitive Klein. Perhaps it is not surprising that he was soon having difficulties at school, playing truant and eventually, in 1946, when he was eighteen, to his everlasting shame failing his baccalaureate exam (an important French exam taken at the same time as A/S levels).

For a while, after leaving school, he had a job working in his aunt's electrical appliance store selling books, which was a side-line of her business. He was desperate to escape the monotony of this existence and at the age of nineteen joined judo classes at the police school in Nice. Here he made an important friendship with Armand Fernandez who, like Klein, would also become an artist.

Klein did his **military service** in Germany and then went to stay in England to learn English. In 1950 he began to think very seriously of becoming an artist. (He had been resisting this occupation because he wanted to be different from his parents.) However, in 1951 he moved to Spain and made a living teaching judo. The following year, with the financial assistance of his aunt, he went to the Kodakan Judo Institute in Tokyo, Japan, which was supposed to be the best in the world. He worked very intensely here and was finally awarded the rank of black belt, higher than any other judo expert in France at that time. However, while in Japan he began to take stimulant drugs, including amphetamines, to help improve his judo performance.

He returned to Paris in 1955, determined to take the judo world by storm. He was bitterly disappointed as the French Judo Federation refused to acknowledge him, even after the publication of his book *Fundamentals of Judo*. They refused to recognize his Japanese qualifications. He decided to go and contemplate his future in Spain. Here he took his first real step towards becoming an artist, preparing a little book of reproductions of non-existent **monochrome** paintings. Each monochrome was back-dated to make it look like he had been working as an artist for a while.

Wild and anarchic, Klein's wayward personality was linked with the strange new art he created.

In 1955, he sent an orange monochrome to the Salon des Réalités Nouvelles in Paris, which was rejected. Undeterred, he arranged a small one-man show of monochromes which was well received by an influential critic, Pierre Restany, who agreed to write the catalogue preface for his next show in 1956. This was a big breakthrough for Klein as it was then that he had the notion of focusing on just one colour – blue, which was to become his trademark. In the 1956 exhibition, he showed canvases, sculptures and other objects all in the same shade of blue. Klein later **patented** the colour as International Klein Blue (IKB).

Leap into the Void, by Yves Klein (1960)
This 'happening' captured on film, records Klein's 'art exhibition' which turned out to be the artist leaping from a first floor window.

It was also in 1956 that Yves Klein met a young art dealer, Iris Clert, who was keen to establish herself as a force in the world of **avant-garde**, experimental art, and saw Klein as a likely candidate for her cause. The second show he held with Clert, in 1958, proved to be his most successful. *Le Vide (The Void)* as it was called consisted of a gallery entrance draped in Klein Blue (of course), flanked by uniformed members of the Republican Guards. After the eager, expectant crowd of nearly 3000 people passed by this grand welcome to the show, they found themselves in a pristine, totally empty, white space. Klein arranged for glasses of blue drink to be offered to those waiting outside. He had put a biologist's stain into the drink so that everyone who drank it had blue urine for a week! The art world, to the delight of both Clert and Klein, was in uproar.

On 5 June 1958, Klein made his first 'living brush' **Performance Art**. For this he directed a nude model, covered in blue paint, to lie down and press the paint onto a canvas on the floor to create a monochrome painting. In February 1960, Klein began his *Anthropométries* where the imprints of the models' bodies were left, as opposed to them covering the whole canvas.

On 27 October 1960, Klein found himself at the centre of a new group put together by the critic Restany. The group was called 'The New Realists'. Their aim was to overcome what they felt was a gap between art and real life. They did this by dealing directly with 'reality', that is the world of the mass media. They used objects from the real world in their art (such as torn advertising posters) and did performances and **happenings** in front of real people.

Klein was by now attracting a good deal of attention. He responded to these new challenges with his customary zeal and energy, but sadly his bouts of elation were accompanied by dangerous mood swings. As he grew more famous, he became increasingly difficult, possibly as a response to the fame and attention, but also as a result of his long-standing addiction to amphetamines, which was now causing him constant insomnia (sleeplessness).

Early in 1961 Klein had a disastrous show at the famous Leo Castelli Gallery in New York. It was slated by the critics and rejected by all the leading New York artists. Back in Paris Klein became preoccupied with death. At the end of 1961, Klein's girlfriend, Rotraut, became pregnant and they married on 21 January 1962. Klein's frail health – mental and physical – was now failing fast. He died from a massive heart attack in Cannes in the South of France on 6 June 1962. He was 34 years old.

Richard Long b. 1945

- Born in Bristol, England, on 2 June 1945.
- Has travelled widely for his work, but still lives in Bristol.

Key works
A Line made by Walking, 1967
Slate Circle, 1979
A Line in Japan, 1979

Richard Long is one of the leading British exponents of **Land Art**. From the late 1960s, he sought to liberate his art from the restriction of the gallery. He was born on 2 June 1945 in Bristol, England. He remembers that as a child he loved walking and the outdoor life. The walks he went on in the countryside around Bristol were very important to his awakening imagination. He later said that he was beginning to make his presence felt in nature mainly by rambling through it.

▌▌ *Long, who first became famous in the 1960s for making installations on the land in the course of his walks, stands in front of one of the pieces he made specifically for a gallery, using natural materials.*

Long studied at the West of England College of Art between 1962 and 1965. During this time he started experimenting with his first Earthworks – works made from natural objects, set in a natural environment.

Long went to London in 1966 to study sculpture at St Martin's College of Art. At that time it was famous for the 'New Sculpture' of welded, painted metal made by artists like Anthony Caro and Philip King, who were the best-known teachers at St Martin's. However, Long already had a strong sense of direction in his art and found himself immediately rebelling against the fashionable ideas of sculpture at St Martin's. He started to make artworks by laying simple materials like sand or water on the floor or the flat roof of the school. He also hit on the idea of using walking as an art form. In 1967, he transported a circle of sticks with a centre line pointing, at the moment of placing, to the sun, from the North of England, where it had been laid out in a field, into a room at St Martin's.

After leaving St Martin's in 1968, Long made a name for himself quite quickly. He had his first one-man show in the Konrad Fischer Gallery in Düsseldorf in 1968. From the beginning he had worked both in the wide open space of landscape and indoors, but now for the first time he had to confront the idea of showing in a gallery, a situation he had never encountered before. 'My art is about working in the wide world,' he said, 'wherever, on the surface of the earth ... My outdoor sculptures and walking locations are not subject to possession and ownership. I like the fact that roads and mountains are common, public land.'

Just a year after his exhibition in Düsseldorf Long was invited to show in Paris, Milan and New York. In 1969 he was included in an influential exhibition entitled 'When Attitude Becomes Form' at the Kunsthalle Bern in Switzerland. After the success of this show Long began creating environmental works all around the world, documenting walks with texts, photographs and maps. In 1989, Long won the **Turner Prize** in London. He still lives in Bristol, his home city, although his work has taken him to far-flung places.

▌▎▎ *Stone Line*, by Richard Long (1978)
Long's materials are always gathered on his walks, like these stones from the Pennines in Yorkshire. They are laid down in careful order according to sketches and diagrams that Long has made.

Henry Moore 1898–86

- Born in Castleford, Yorkshire, on 30 July 1898.
- Died Much Hadham, Hertfordshire, on 31 August 1986.

Key works

Reclining Figure, 1929
Family Group, 1948
Stringed Figure, 1956

Henry Moore was the most celebrated 20th-century British sculptor. He was one of the first sculptors who specifically wanted his work to be sited out of doors, so that each piece would have a direct relationship with the surrounding landscape. He was also strongly motivated by nature. In this sense he was an early Land or Earth artist, for whom the whole planet was his studio.

Henry Moore was born on 30 July 1898 in Castleford, Yorkshire. He was the seventh of eight children. His father was a mine manager. He believed in education and was encouraging and supportive to his son, who showed unusual gifts at an early age. Moore was later to remember his childhood as a very happy time.

From 1914, many qualified teachers had to join the army to fight in World War I. Moore became a student teacher in 1915 and by 1916 he was teaching in the primary school which he had attended as a boy. At seventeen, he joined the army in the Civil Service Rifles. He had a relatively easy time, unlike many less fortunate, later describing army life as being 'just like a bigger family'. He used his time in London to visit the British Museum and the National Gallery. In 1917 he was sent to Cambrai in Northern France where he was gassed and had to spend three months in hospital recovering. After leaving the hospital he was made a physical training instructor and then was finally discharged from the army in February 1919.

In September 1919, after a brief return to primary school teaching, Moore decided to pursue his growing passion for art and enrolled at Leeds College of Art. His talent was soon noticed and he was given a **scholarship** to the Royal College of Art in London. Later, he recalled the intense excitement he felt going to London: 'I was in a dream of excitement. When I rode on top of a bus I felt that I was travelling in Heaven. And that the bus was floating in air.'

Moore loved looking at all the art of the past in London. Later he was exposed to the art of Italy, when he visited that country on a travelling scholarship from the Royal College of Art in 1925. Returning from Italy he took up a part-time post as Assistant in the Sculpture Department at the Royal College of Art. In 1926, still in his twenties, he had his first one-man show. He was also commissioned to provide a sculpture for the headquarters of the London Underground, above St James's Park tube station.

In 1929, Moore married a beautiful Russian woman named Irina Radetsky. Together they bought a small cottage in Kent and Moore was able to work during the College holidays. He was now working towards his second one-man exhibition, which eventually received very mixed reviews, even though the famous sculptor Jacob Epstein had written the catalogue introduction stating that 'for the future of sculpture in England Moore is vitally important'. As Moore was now becoming an increasingly controversial figure, the conservative Royal College decided not to renew his teaching contract. The more forward-looking Chelsea College of Art approached him, however, and he took up a teaching post there.

Towards the end of his long life, when this photograph was taken of the artist surrounded by his work, Moore had achieved world-wide recognition for his sculpture.

Family Group, by Henry Moore (1946)
After the birth of his daughter in 1946, the year this sculpture was made, Moore became preoccupied with more representative depictions of the human form, often focusing on family groups, such as this bronze sculpture. After the appalling suffering in the aftermath of World War II, these works came to represent hope for continued life.

A couple of years later in 1934, the Moores moved to another cottage in Kent, which was not actually larger, but had five acres of land attached. This gave Moore the opportunity to display his work in the open, which was becoming increasingly important to him. However, the Moores then decided to move back to London, to be in the midst of the art world again. They lived in Hampstead and became part of a group of artists that included the painter Ben Nicholson and the sculptor Barbara Hepworth, whom Moore had previously met at Leeds College of Art. They were to have an important friendship and exchange of artistic ideas.

During World War II Chelsea College of Art was evacuated. Moore applied to Chelsea Polytechnic for training as a munitions toolmaker. It was during this period that he began to make his celebrated drawings of people sheltering in the London Underground from the bombing during the Blitz. These drawings showed another side of Moore's artistic personality. He was clearly a brilliant draughtsman (someone who makes detailed technical drawings), but there is also tremendous humanity and compassion in these drawings, not always so discernible in his sculpture. The War Artists Advisory Committee saw the drawings and commissioned Moore to make finished versions that were shown to the public in 1940.

Moore's Hampstead house was badly damaged during an air raid. He decided to move to a village in Hertfordshire – Much Hadham – which would become his home until the end of his life. Here, after the war, he built an experimental **foundry** in his gardens. This foundry provided an opportunity for many assistants to come and help with his larger works, something for which Moore would later be criticized. The view at that time was that artists should do all the work themselves.

It was in his foundry that Moore carried out his famous **commission** in 1943 for St Matthew's Church in Northampton, *Virgin and Child*, which sparked off a whole series of mother and child images. These were doubtless partly inspired by the birth of Moore's first child, a daughter, in 1946.

Moore was well on the way to being recognized internationally in 1946 when New York's Museum of Modern Art gave him a **retrospective**, which was a huge success. Two years later, in 1948, Moore was asked to represent Britain at the **Venice Biennale**, where he was awarded the main sculpture prize.

For the next 40 years until his death at Much Hadham on 31 August 1986, Moore was to enjoy a huge and sustained success. Honours, including the Order of Merit, were bestowed upon him. After the war he turned way from **abstract** work and, responding to the climate of feeling in a ravaged, post-war Britain, returned to the human form, often depicting family groups that celebrated the richness and continuity of life. Executed in a wide range of media – bronze, stone, marble and plaster – they became more ambitious and larger in scale, so that the outdoor world became their best setting.

Claes Oldenburg b. 1929

- Born in Stockholm, Sweden, on 28 January 1929.
- Has lived in the USA since the age of seven.

Key works

Bedroom Ensemble, 1963
Soft Drainpipe – Blue Cool Version, 1967
Spoonbridge and Cherry, 1988

Claes Oldenburg first came to wide attention as one of the leading figures of American **Pop Art** in the early 1960s. However, as he continued to reinvent himself, he also became a very early pioneer of environmental or **Installation Art**. He was born in Stockholm on 28 January 1929, the eldest of two sons of the Swedish Consul-General. When Oldenburg was seven, the family moved to Chicago, USA, after his father was appointed consul there.

As a Swedish immigrant, Oldenburg spoke no English, so during his early years in the USA, he helped to overcome his feeling of isolation by escaping into his own strange fantasy world. He invented an imaginary island which he called 'Neubern', where the language was half-Swedish and half-English. He carefully documented all aspects of this country in a series of scrapbooks. These contain many images that were to recur later in his art. 'Everything I do is original,' he said. 'I made it all up when I was a little kid.'

He went to Chicago Latin School for boys, but found it somewhat stuffy. In 1946, he went to Yale University, where he concentrated on literature and art but also took a drama course. He returned to Chicago in 1950, and began work as a junior reporter with the City News Bureau. It was only after he was rejected from the army a couple of years later that he decided to become an artist and began attending classes at the Art Institute of Chicago. Eventually he decided that New York was the place to be so left Chicago in June 1956.

▮▮▮ *The artist sits in his studio surrounded by some of his food sculptures, like the cheese burger. Initially associated with the Pop Art movement in New York in the 1960s, Oldenburg went on to reinvent himself several times.*

Oldenburg took a job shelving books at the Cooper Union Museum and Art School, and took the opportunity to learn more about art. At the same time he maintained an interest in the world of theatre. He got to know a group of environmental artists, and through them he was asked to co-found a gallery in the Judson Memorial Church. This was used for dance, theatre and poetry events, as well as for showing experimental work by new artists. Oldenburg had his first exhibition there in May and June 1959.

In September 1962, Oldenburg had a show in the Green Gallery. For this his wife Pat, whom he had married in 1960, helped him to stitch his first giant soft sculptures of familiar domestic appliances and products – there was a 2.7-metre cake and a hamburger 2 metres in diameter. His work was by now attracting a good deal of attention. It was also increasing in size, which led to more and more of it being displayed outside. His 1976 *Clothespin,* for example, is on display surrounded by the skyscrapers of Philadelphia's city centre.

In his later life as an artist, Oldenburg has continued to make large-scale projects and performances. Together with his second wife Coosje van Bruggen, a former museum curator whom he married in 1977, Oldenburg creates gigantic sculptures which have become part of strange performances staged all over the great cities of Europe. He now lives in New York.

▮▮▮ *Bedroom Ensemble,* by Claes Oldenburg (1963)
Bedroom Ensemble is a full-scale, bedroom suite that was designed during a seven-month stay in California, in 1963–64, when he began to develop ideas on the theme of the home. It was inspired by a Malibu motel room he stayed in during a visit in 1947.

David Smith 1906–65

- Born in Decatur, Indiana, USA, on 9 March 1906.
- Died in a car crash in Albany, New York, on 23 May 1965.

Key works

Home of the Welder, 1945
Untitled, Zik VI, 1964
Cub XIX, 1964

David Smith was one of the most original and internationally influential American sculptors of the 20th century. He was born on 9 March 1906 at Decatur, Indiana, USA. His father managed a local telephone company but in his spare time was an (unsuccessful) inventor. His mother was a teacher, with a dominant personality and strong religious views. David was always very adventurous and independent, running off to his grandmother's house when he got fed up at home. The illustrations in the Bible that she gave him seemed to have given him the idea of becoming an artist. Once, when he was only three, his mother tied him to a tree to stop him from escaping. Whilst he was kept prisoner, he modelled a lion from the surrounding mud – his first work of art!

In 1921, when Smith was fifteen, the family moved to Paulding, Ohio. He studied mechanical drawing for two years at high school and followed a correspondence course in art with Cleveland Art School. In 1924, he spent an unhappy year at Ohio University, and passed the following summer working at the Studebaker car factory in South Bend. His experience at the car factory gave Smith a basic knowledge of factory tools and equipment, which was very important for his future work. It was his first exposure to working men: he found that he instantly identified and empathized with their hard lives and felt happier with them than with anyone he had met in his college days. 'I know workmen, their vision,' he later said, 'because between college years I have worked on Studebaker's production line.'

The next years were rather restless for Smith. After his summer at the factory, he attended the University of Notre Dame, Indiana, for just two weeks before he moved to Washington, DC. In 1926 he worked for a bank, Acceptance Corporation, which transferred him to New York. Here he met Dorothy Dehner, who would later become his wife. She suggested he enrol at the **Art Students' League**. They got to know the summer resort of Bolton Landing, on the western side of Lake George through friends at the League. They bought a property there, soon after they were married on Christmas Eve 1927.

Through his sculpture, Smith linked Cubist and Surrealist imagery with the technological power of American industry.

Smith was a painting student but his teacher, who was a sculptor, encouraged him to experiment with texture and relief (a way of cutting into a material so that parts of it stand out from the rest). Around 1930 Smith discovered the welded sculpture of Pablo Picasso and Julio Gonzalez through reproductions. In 1932 Smith bought his own welding equipment, but he kept setting fire to the curtains when using it in his Brooklyn apartment. His wife suggested he ask at a neighbouring ironworks, Terminal Ironworks, for working space. They agreed, and Smith forged a relationship with the men in charge and their friends, who used to meet nearby at a men-only salon. 'It was the social hall for blocks around,' Smith later remembered. 'Any method or technique I needed I could learn it from one of the habitués (frequent visitors) and often get donated material besides.' At this stage, Smith was also developing a keen interest in left-wing politics, aided and abetted by his friend, the artist John Graham. It was Graham who suggested the three of them should set sail for Europe in 1935. He introduced them to important artists in Paris, before they sailed on to Greece and the Soviet Union.

■■■ *Wagon II*, by David Smith (1964)
Smith's early experience working in a car factory gave him invaluable experience of factory tools and equipment which later helped inform ambitious iron works such as Wagon II.

Back in the States, Smith established a pattern of spending the summer at Bolton Landing and returning to New York for the winter, working for the **New Deal** art programme. He was becoming increasingly committed to **abstract** art, which he believed could be developed to express political and social ideas. 'The great majority of abstract artists,' he claimed around 1940, 'are anti-fascist and socially conscious.'

Although Smith was gradually beginning to gain recognition for his work, he was still not making money from it. In 1940, he left New York and went to work as a machinist at Glen Falls, then as a welder in the American Locomotive Company Plant at Schenectady. 'Figured I better get a job — so I went down to Schenectady to employment office — hired in a welder — got stuck with the graveyard shift,' Smith wrote. 'This new studio I built, I christened the Terminal Iron Works — partly because the change in my particular type of sculpture required a factory more than an 'Atelier' [studio]. When I went to Schenectady I found it very difficult to make art when physical labor was so strenuous ...'

After World War II Smith returned to Bolton Landing where he and his wife built a house, virtually single-handed. Sadly, however, the marriage began to fail. Smith was drinking heavily and was prone to fits of temper when he was drunk. His wife divorced him in 1950, accusing him of wife-beating. Smith was struggling with a broken marriage and all the insecurities of trying to become recognized as an artist. Yet he had tremendous faith in the value of his art. Even in his most depressed times he was able to write, 'I believe that my time is the most important in the world — that the art of my time is the most important art.'

On 6 April 1953, now in his late forties, Smith married again. Jean Freas bore him two daughters, one in 1954 and one in 1955, but by 1958 the marriage had begun to fall apart. Smith was on his own again. He became increasingly melancholic, though comforted a little by the beginnings of a much wider recognition of his work. In 1957 the Museum of Modern Art in New York held a major **retrospective** of his work. In 1962, the Italian government invited him to spend a month at Voltri, near Genoa, making an abandoned factory and several workmen available to him. He made 27 huge sculptures in 30 days, works which would later help to establish his international reputation.

Although in the last few years of his life Smith had achieved everything he set out to do, his solitary nature isolated him, with drink his only constant companion. On 23 May 1965, aged 59, he was killed in an accident while driving his pick-up truck in Benington, late at night.

Rachel Whiteread b. 1963

- Born in London on 20 April 1963.
- Has lived in London most of her life.

Key works

Untitled (Airbed), 1992
Untitled (Floor/Ceiling), 1993
Untitled (Floor), 1994–5

It was Rachel Whiteread's *House*, a temporary public sculpture in Bow, East London, that first made her famous. She was born in London on 20 April 1963. She is the youngest of three girls; her twin sisters, Karen and Lynne are two years older than her. Her father, who died in 1989 when Whiteread was still a student, taught geography at the former North East London Polytechnic. Her mother, Pat Whiteread, who has been a big influence in Whiteread's life, is a multi-media artist, who has campaigned for better recognition for women artists.

When she was a toddler, Whiteread remembers her mother painting in her studio at home. Whiteread's job was to sharpen pencils. 'She was a very good mother, there is no doubt about it,' she says. 'But I think like many women she was pulled in different directions.' As a mother of small children, work brought her a sense of fulfilment and also frustration. She seriously wanted to become an artist but sometimes her frustrations were taken out on her children and husband. 'My father was genuinely very supportive but there were difficulties, and they both had health problems too,' she remembers.

Whiteread's parents were opposites. Her father was very down-to-earth and steady and her mother was more volatile. 'From my mother I've inherited creativity, tenacity – stubbornness perhaps. From my father I think I've inherited a level-headedness.'

The family lived in Essex when the children were young so that they could be near the countryside. 'I now think this was incredibly generous of my parents, although it was quite an alienating experience for my mother. Ever since we were small she would take us to all kinds of museums and galleries and contemporary exhibitions.'

When Whiteread was seven the family decided to move back to Muswell Hill, London. It was a very diplomatic household with washing-up rotas and the girls went to the local comprehensive.

For a long time Whiteread rejected the idea of going into art – possibly a reaction to her parents – and she had always concentrated on the sciences. 'My mum had exhibitions, and I felt very proud of her, if a bit confused. At the private views I wasn't quite sure who all those people were by the end as everyone got drunker and the volume got louder.'

Whiteread was fourteen when her mother became one of a group of women selecting work for 'Women's Images of Men', which was a very important show at the ICA (Institute of Contemporary Arts). It was **feminist** art, innovative and powerful and very much what was happening in the 1970s. 'Had it not been for my mother's generation of artists and their achievements, I wouldn't be in the position I am today. Things have moved on. I think my mother changed her mind about some of that art, finding it too aggressive. But she was a good role model.'

▌▌▌ *The first woman to win the Turner Prize in 1993, Whiteread would be the first to admit she was fortunate to be recognized for her highly original work comparatively early on in her career.*

■■ *House*, by Rachel Whiteread (1993–94)
Although now demolished, this sculpture of the negative space of a Victorian
house became something of a landmark in London's East End during its brief life.

Later in her teens, Whiteread felt she had done enough academically and decided she wanted to do a foundation course at art school. She did 'A' level art in one year and got a grade B. After she left art school in 1989, her father died of heart failure.

Whiteread's first exhibition was two months after the death of her father. She had been very inward-looking and found herself dwelling on the subject of death. Some of her early work is autobiographical. For example, in *Closet*, which was the interior of a wardrobe covered in black felt, Whiteread looks back to her childhood after the end of World War II by using a kind of furniture common at that time called 'utilitarian' furniture.

Whiteread casts space, giving solidity to things that were once invisible. The idea of making sculpture of the negative aspects of an object was originally invented by the American artist Bruce Nauman (b. 1941) who cast the underside of a single chair. Whiteread has been influenced both by Nauman's work and the American **Installation Artist** Robert Gober (b. 1954), whose plaster sinks were shown at the Saatchi Collection's New York Art exhibition in 1987/88. But Whiteread has explored the concept of casting negative space in the context of the UK and a fascination with domestic life. Her sculptures often have a very simple appearance, plain, pale and box-like. When she casts in plaster, however, her sinks, baths and mattresses look classical and rather majestic, like tombs or sarcophagi (stone coffins).

In 1993, there was a huge public debate about whether or not her sculpture, *House*, a concrete cast of the interior of an old terraced house, should be demolished or kept. In the end, to many people's lasting disappointment, it was demolished. 'Although I was obviously sorry when *House* was pulled down, I also felt very proud about the interest it generated,' Whiteread said. 'I felt it had done its job in making people aware of the power a modern work of art can have. The local council's decision to pull it down also underlined the deep suspicion of contemporary art in this country.'

Whiteread has strong socialist ideals that she feels are reflected in her work. 'I've lived in London most of my life and growing up in the Thatcher years, seeing the deprivation and more and more homeless people everywhere, I feel very sad about what is happening here, you see things crumble around you and you're helpless to do anything.'

Although Whiteread has always insisted that she is not a radical artist 'standing on my soap box', no recent contemporary sculpture has been so suggestive of the 1990s as *House*. She often refers to London as her 'sketchbook'. In that same year, Whiteread became the first woman to win the **Turner Prize**. This achievement confirmed her as a leading light on the British art scene.

Timeline

1898   Henry Moore born 30 July

1903   Barbara Hepworth born 10 January

1906   David Smith born 9 March

1911   Louise Bourgeois born 24 December

1913   *Bicycle Wheel*, the first 'ready-made' produced by Marcel Duchamp

1914–18   World War I

1921   Joseph Beuys born 12 May

1928   Yves Klein born 28 April

1929   Claes Oldenburg born 28 January

1935   Christo born 13 June

1939   Outbreak of World War II

1944   Rebecca Horn born 24 March

1945   End of World War II; Richard Long born 2 June

1947	Institute of Contemporary Art established in London
1948	Henry Moore wins main sculpture prize at the Venice Biennale
1950	Anthony Gormley born
1956	Andy Goldsworthy born
1959	The **Happenings** start to take place in New York, USA
1960	Jean-Michel Basquiat born 22 December
1963	Rachel Whiteread born 20 April
1979	Margaret Thatcher became Prime Minister
1982	Falklands War
1984	First **Turner Prize** awarded to celebrate British art
1991	Gulf War
1993	Rachel Whiteread becomes first woman to win the Turner Prize

Glossary

abstract art removed from the recognizable. In terms of an art work it is not recognizable as an object, landscape, or person. A work where colour and shape are more important than what they represent.

Art Students' League set up in 1895, the League holds courses for small groups of artists to learn techniques from other artists

avant-garde pioneers or innovators in any sphere of the arts

bohemian unconventional; someone who lives in an informal, flamboyant way

collage a piece of art made up of a variety of different materials – cuttings from newspapers, string or fabric for example

commission piece of work specifically requested by a group or art collector

Cubism early 20th-century school of painting and sculpture in which objects are shown as abstract geometric forms without realistic detail; often involving transparent cubes and cones

École des Beaux-Arts (School of Fine Arts) official art school financed and run by the French government. The most prestigious was L'École Nationale Supérieure des Beaux-Arts in Paris. Founded in 1648, the teaching was very conservative.

empaquetage art form which consists in wrapping objects, some of them – for example, buildings or whole landscapes – very large

Environmental Art type of art where the viewer is able to enter the three-dimensional space and be included in the art work. The idea for this first appeared in a manifesto by the Russian artist Wassily Kandinsky, but the Surrealist artists were the first to produce work using the idea.

feminist movement movement that emerged in the 1960s to fight for equal rights for women

figurative art art in which recognizable figures or objects are portrayed

foundry a factory where metal is moulded and used to produce other things

graffiti writing or drawings on a wall or other public area, often in spray paint

happening performance carried out by an artist; originated in New York, 1959

Installation Art term first coined in the 1960s to describe works that are not displayed as individual objects in an exhibition. Often these works are designed for a specific room which the viewer can enter and be a part of. An installation may involve video, paintings, sculptures or photographs.

kinetic of or relating to motion

Land Art art that has been constructed outside of the gallery or museum, in the countryside, using 'found' material, such as leaves or stones

menhir a standing stone from pre-historic times

military service legal requirement for all men over school leaving age to serve for a year or more in the armed services

monochrome painting or drawing in tones of only one colour

New Deal project set up by the US government in the 1930s to provide work for artists (and others)

patent official right of an inventor to produce or sell his or her own invention for a set amount of time without it being copied

Performance Art work of art as an isolated museum piece is replaced with creative action to establish a new relationship between artist and audience and also, by implication, between art and life

Pop Art movement that originated in New York, USA in the 1950s and 60s. It took commercialism and the media as its basis.

Post-modern art that was produced after the 1960s

retrospective an exhibition which shows an artist's work over his or her lifetime

salon annual exhibition of the French Royal Academy of Painting and Sculpture

scholarship when a student is given a sum of money in order to continue his or her studies

scrim an open weave material that is used to produce special effects on stage

stereotype a person or thing that represents a conventional type

Surrealism movement originally developed in Paris in 1921 that aimed to express the subconscious mind by the use of bizarre, irrational, absurd and dreamlike images

Turner Prize art competition set up in 1984 by the Patrons of New Art and the Tate Gallery 'to bring new developments in the visual arts to the attention of people who are interested in the culture of our time'. Four artists, under the age of 35, are chosen every autumn to show their work in an exhibition at the Tate Gallery. The winner receives a cheque for £20,000.

Venice Biennale international exhibition of contemporary art that takes place every two years in Venice, Italy. Has been held regularly since 1895.

Video Art began in the 1960s as a response to the increasing popularity of television. In the 1980s the borderline between video art and popular commercial video became blurred. In the 1990s there was a tendency to merge video and computer art. Its combination with sculptural elements has established it as an art form in its own right.

Whitney Biennial celebration of American contemporary art first seen in 1932. Every two years the Bucksbaum Award is presented to an artist showing work at the exhibition.

Resources

LIST OF FAMOUS WORKS

Jean-Michel Basquiat (1960–88)
Untitled, 1981
K, 1982
Napoleonic Stereotype, 1983
Zydeco, 1984

Joseph Beuys (1921–86)
Bed, 1950
Felt Suit, 1970
The Revolution is Us, 1972

Louise Bourgeois (b. 1911)
The Destruction of the Father, 1973
Eyes, 1982
Cell (Eyes and Mirrors), 1989
Woman and Suitcase, 1994

Christo (b. 1935)
Wrapped Coast – One Million Square Feet (Little Bay, Australia), 1969
Valley Curtain (Rifle, Colorado), 1972
Running Fence, 1976

Andy Goldsworthy (b. 1956)
Balanced Rocks, 1978
Maple Leaf Lines, 1987
Conical Leafwork, 1988
Leadgate Maze, 1989

Anthony Gormley (b. 1950)
Untitled (For Francis), 1986
Angel of the North, 1998
Quantum Cloud, 2000

Barbara Hepworth (1903–75)
Three Forms, 1934
Pelagos, 1946
Curved Form, 1956
Merryn, 1962
Hollow Form with Inner Form, 1968

Rebecca Horn (b. 1944)
Ballet of the Woodpeckers, 1986
Orlando, 1988
Concert for Anarchy, 1990

Yves Klein (1928–62)
Do–Do–Do Blue, 1960
Leap into the Void, 1960
FC –11 Anthropometry-Fire, 1961

Richard Long (b. 1945)
A Line made by Walking, 1967
Slate Circle, 1979
A Line in Japan, 1979
Thirty-seven Campfires, Mexico, 1987

Henry Moore (1893–1986)
Reclining Figure, 1929
Family Group, 1948
Stringed Figure, 1956
Large Two Forms, 1966-69

Claes Oldenburg (b. 1929)
Bedroom Ensemble, 1963
Soft Toilet, 1966
Soft Drainpipe – Blue Cool Version, 1967
Spoonbridge and Cherry, 1988

David Smith (1906–65)
Home of the Welder, 1945
Untitled, Zik V1, 1964
Cub X1X, 1964

Rachel Whiteread (b. 1960)
Untitled (Airbed), 1992
Untitled (Floor/Ceiling), 1993
House, 1993-94
Untitled (Floor), 1994–5

Further reading

General

Art Since 1960, Michael Archer, Thames and Hudson, 2002 (second edition)

Lives of the Great 20th-Century Artists, Edward Lucie-Smith, Thames and Hudson, 1999

New Media in Late 20th-Century Art, Michael Rush, Thames and Hudson, 1999

The History of Art, Claudio Merle, Hodder Wayland

The History of Western Painting, Juliet Heslewood, Belitha Press

The History of Western Sculpture, Juliet Heslewood, Belitha Press

20th Century Art: 1980–2000 Very Modern Art, Clare Oliver, 2000, Heinemann Library

Understanding Modern Art, M Bohm-Duchen and J Cook, Usborne Publishing

The artists

Basquiat, Phoebe Hoban, Quartet Books, 1998

Joseph Beuys, Norman Rosenthal, Heiner Bastian, Royal Academy of Arts, 1999

The Essential Joseph Beuys, Alain Borer, Thames and Hudson, 1997

Louise Bourgeois, Frances Morris, Tate Gallery Publishing, 2000

Midsummer Snowballs, Andy Goldsworthy, Thames and Hudson, 2001

Time – Andy Goldsworthy, Andy Goldsworthy, Thames and Hudson, 2000

Making an Angel, Anthony Gormley, Booth-Clibborn Editions, 1998

Barbara Hepworth, Penelope Curtis, Tate Gallery Publishing, 1998

Barbara Hepworth, Matthew Gale, Chris Stephens, Tate Gallery Publishing, 1999

Richard Long: Walking in Circles, Anne Seymour (Introduction), Thames and Hudson, 1994

Richard Long, William Malpas, Crescent Moon Publishing, 1995

Henry Moore, Jeremy Wallis, Heinemann Library, 2002

Claes Oldenburg, Ellen Hulda Johnson, Penguin, 1971

The Fields of David Smith, Candida Smith, Irving Sandler, Thames & Hudson, 1999

Rachel Whiteread's House, John Bird, et al, James Lingwood (Editor), Phaidon Press, 1995

Where to see Contemporary Art

UK
Gallery of Modern Art, Glasgow

Hayward Gallery, London
www.hayward.org.uk
Manchester Art Gallery, Manchester
www.manchestergalleries.org
Tate Modern, London
www.tate.org.uk/modern

White Cube Gallery, London
www.whitecube.com

USA
Museum of Contemporary Art, Los Angeles
moca-la.org/index.php

Museum of Modern Art, New York
www.moma.org

New Museum of Contemporary Art, New York
www.newmuseum.org

Smithsonian American Art Museum, Washington
nmaa-ryder.si.edu

Index